Buy Low To Build High

How To Identify And Capitalize On Undervalued Investment Opportunities

By

Kerri Payne

Kerri Payne

Copyright © 2024, Kerri Payne
All Rights Reserved.

Except for brief quotations included in critical reviews and other non-commercial uses allowed by copyright law, no part of this publication may be duplicated, distributed, or transmitted in any way without the publisher's prior written consent. This includes photocopies, recordings, and other electronic or mechanical methods. For permission requests, send a letter to the publisher.

The suggestions and tactics offered in the writing might not apply in all circumstances. It is understood that neither the author nor the publisher will be held liable for the outcomes of using the recommendations in this book.

Kerri Payne

Table Of Contents

Introduction

1. **Value Investing and Undervalued Assets**
   - Undervaluation, Subjectivity & Efficient Markets
   - Value Investing vs. Values-Based Investing

2. **Identifying Potential Opportunities Through Market Analysis**
   - Assessing The Intrinsic Value Of An Investment

3. **Using Charts And Patterns To Spot Undervalued Assets**
   - Uncovering Hidden Value Through Financial Analysis

4. **Recognizing Game-Changing Trends And**

Kerri Payne

<u>Their Potential Impact</u>
- <u>Assessing The Leadership And Track Record Of A Company</u>
- <u>Weighing Potential Risks And Rewards Of An Investment</u>

<u>5. Spreading Risk Across Different Asset Classes And Industries</u>
- <u>Staying Updated On Current Events That Can Impact Investment Opportunities</u>

<u>Conclusion</u>

Kerri Payne

Introduction

"Undervalued" is a financial term that describes a security or investment that is trading at a market price believed to be less than its actual intrinsic value. The intrinsic value of a company is calculated as the present value of the expected future free cash flows it will generate. To determine if a stock is undervalued, one can examine the company's financial statements and analyze its fundamentals, such as cash flow, return on assets, profit generation, and capital management, to estimate the stock's intrinsic value.

On the other hand, a stock considered overvalued is one that is trading in the market at a price higher than its perceived value. Purchasing stocks when they are undervalued is a fundamental aspect of renowned investor Warren Buffett's value investing strategy.

However, value investing is not without its flaws. There is no certainty regarding when or if an undervalued stock will increase in value. Additionally, accurately determining a stock's intrinsic value is challenging and largely involves educated guesses. When someone claims a stock is undervalued, they are essentially stating their belief that the stock's true worth exceeds its current market price. This assessment is inherently subjective and might not always be based on a rational analysis of the company's fundamentals.

A stock considered undervalued is believed to be priced too low according to current indicators used in valuation models. If a company's stock is significantly lower than the industry average, it might be deemed undervalued. Value investors may target these stocks, aiming to achieve reasonable returns at a lower initial cost.

Determining whether a stock is truly undervalued is subjective. An inaccurate or improperly applied valuation model could indicate that the stock is already fairly valued.

This book educates readers on identifying undervalued investment opportunities through fundamental and technical analysis. It emphasizes risk management strategies, including diversification and staying informed about market trends and current events. Practical examples illustrate successful approaches to capitalize on undervalued assets across various industries and market conditions.

Kerri Payne

Kerri Payne

1

Value Investing and Undervalued Assets

Value investing is an investment strategy that seeks out undervalued stocks or securities in the market, aiming to buy them at lower prices to enhance the potential for returns.

Moreover, this approach steers clear of purchasing items perceived as overvalued to avoid potential negative returns.

Kerri Payne

Undervaluation, Subjectivity & Efficient Markets

The concept that a stock can consistently be undervalued or overvalued, allowing investors to consistently earn above-average returns by trading on these mispricings, contradicts the notion of market efficiency where all available information is fully utilized.

If a stock's true intrinsic value is significantly higher than its market price and this information is easily identifiable from its financial statements, all market participants would be motivated to buy the stock, thereby pushing its price up to reflect its intrinsic value.

In essence, if markets are efficient, identifying a genuinely undervalued stock should be exceedingly difficult (unless one possesses

Kerri Payne

non-public information). This suggests that an investor who believes a particular stock is undervalued is essentially making a subjective assessment that goes against the consensus of the market, barring insider knowledge. Furthermore, the existence of successful value traders who consistently outperform the market poses a challenge to the theory of market efficiency.

Values-based investing, unlike value investing which seeks undervalued stocks, involves purchasing shares in companies aligned with an investor's personal beliefs and values. This strategy prioritizes personal convictions over potential profitability indicated by market metrics.

For instance, an investor might avoid investing in tobacco companies but favor renewable energy firms based on their ethical stance. This approach underscores the investor's consideration of whether a company's products and industry align with their individual values.

Value Investing vs. Values-Based Investing

Values-based investing involves purchasing shares in companies that align with an investor's personal values, distinct from value investing which seeks undervalued stocks. This strategy allows investors to make investment decisions based on their personal beliefs, regardless of whether market indicators suggest profitability.

It may involve avoiding investments in companies whose products are not supported by the investor's values and instead allocating funds to companies that are in line with their beliefs.

For instance, if an investor opposes cigarette smoking but favors alternative fuel sources, they would allocate their investments accordingly. This approach to investing suggests that the investor prioritizes alignment with their personal values when considering both the product and industry sectors.

Kerri Payne

Kerri Payne

2

Identifying Potential Opportunities Through Market Analysis

A key aspect of identifying undervalued investment prospects involves conducting comprehensive market analysis. By analyzing market trends, you can discover potential opportunities that may have been overlooked by others.

Start by monitoring the performance of different industries. Identify sectors that are experiencing growth or emerging trends that could potentially increase valuations.

Understanding the dynamics of supply and demand within an industry can provide valuable insights into potential investment prospects. For example, if there is increasing demand for a particular product or service but limited market supply, it may signal an opportunity for investment that is undervalued.

Macroeconomic indicators such as interest rates, inflation, and GDP growth have a significant impact on investment valuations. Monitoring these factors helps in identifying sectors or assets that are undervalued due to broader market sentiments.

Sentiment analysis involves evaluating the overall mood and perception of market participants. Assessing sentiment enables investors to pinpoint instances where excessive fear or pessimism has led to undervaluation of assets.

For instance, during economic downturns or market volatility, many investors sell off their holdings due to fear, resulting in price declines. Analyzing market sentiment allows savvy investors to spot undervalued opportunities amid these panic-driven sell-offs.

Assessing The Intrinsic Value Of An Investment

Fundamental analysis involves examining the essential factors that influence a company's intrinsic value. By focusing on critical financial metrics, industry position, and growth prospects, investors can determine whether an investment is undervalued relative to its true worth.

Reviewing a company's earnings and cash flow statements helps assess its financial stability and growth potential. Seek out consistent revenue growth and positive cash flow, indicators of a healthy and undervalued investment opportunity.

Analyzing a company's balance sheet provides insights into its financial structure, assets, and liabilities. A robust balance sheet with minimal debt may indicate an undervalued investment opportunity.

Assess a company's competitive advantage and market position to determine its potential for long-term growth. Companies that maintain sustainable competitive advantages often present attractive opportunities for undervalued investments.

Kerri Payne

Compare a company's valuation metrics, such as price-to-earnings (P/E) ratio or price-to-book (P/B) ratio, with those of its industry peers. If a company shows lower valuation metrics relative to competitors despite similar growth prospects, it may signal an undervalued investment opportunity.

For example, imagine analyzing the automobile sector and discovering a company with strong growth prospects, a healthy balance sheet, and lower valuation metrics compared to its peers. This scenario suggests a potential undervalued investment opportunity warranting further examination.

Kerri Payne

Kerri Payne

3

Using Charts And Patterns To Spot Undervalued Assets

Technical analysis utilizes historical price and volume data to forecast future price movements, contrasting with fundamental analysis which focuses on assessing the intrinsic value of investments. By analyzing market trends and patterns, technical analysis aids in identifying undervalued assets.

Identify price levels where an asset frequently encounters support or resistance. Consistent rebounding from a support level suggests a potential undervalued opportunity when the price nears that level.

Observe indicators of trend changes, such as shifts in moving average directions or the formation of chart patterns like double bottoms or head and shoulders. Early detection of these signals can help identify undervalued assets.

Utilize technical indicators like the Relative Strength Index (RSI) or Moving Average Convergence Divergence (MACD) to pinpoint instances of oversold or overbought conditions. An oversold asset might be undervalued, indicating a possible upcoming price correction.

Volume analysis involves evaluating trading volume alongside price fluctuations. A substantial increase in volume during price declines may suggest panic selling, presenting potential opportunities for undervalued investments.

For example, in stock market analysis, if a specific stock displays a classic double bottom pattern near a significant support level, it could signify that the stock is undervalued and potentially primed for an upward price movement.

Uncovering Hidden Value Through Financial Analysis

Financial statements are essential for investors seeking to uncover hidden value within a company. By analyzing financial ratios, cash flow patterns, and profitability metrics, investors can identify opportunities where investments may be undervalued.

Kerri Payne

Evaluate a company's profitability indicators, such as return on equity (ROE) and gross profit margin, to assess its profit generation capability. Stronger profitability metrics compared to industry benchmarks could suggest potential undervaluation.

Review a company's cash flow statements to gauge its ability to generate consistent cash flows. Positive cash flow positions the company well to pursue growth initiatives, potentially signaling undervalued investment prospects.

Consider a company's debt-to-equity ratio and interest coverage ratio to assess its financial stability and ability to manage debt. A manageable debt load and a healthy interest coverage ratio may suggest an investment opportunity that is undervalued.

Kerri Payne

Compare a company's financial ratios with those of its industry peers to identify disparities. If a company demonstrates solid financial performance but trades at a lower valuation than similar competitors, it may represent an appealing investment opportunity.

For instance, in the retail sector, suppose you find a company with strong profitability, robust cash flows, and minimal debt. Despite these strengths, its stock price is significantly discounted compared to other companies in the same industry. This scenario could indicate an undervalued investment opportunity within the retail sector.

Kerri Payne

Kerri Payne

Recognizing Game-Changing Trends And Their Potential Impact

The investment environment is continuously changing, driven by new technologies and disruptive innovations. Recognizing industry disruptions helps investors identify sectors or companies that may be undervalued and poised to benefit from these transformative trends.

Monitor emerging technologies and their potential impact across different industries. Look for companies that are positioning themselves to capitalize on these advancements but have not yet gained full recognition from the market.

Changes in regulations or government policies can create opportunities for undervalued investments. Staying informed about regulatory developments allows investors to pinpoint sectors where the market has not fully priced in the potential effects of new regulations.

Evaluate the sustainability of current business models within industries. Companies with disruptive business models that challenge traditional norms may present undervalued investment opportunities.

Identifying emerging trends enables investors to pinpoint undervalued prospects in developing industries or those undergoing significant changes. For instance, the growth of electric vehicles or the adoption of renewable energy sources offers potential undervalued investment opportunities.

Consider a scenario where you discover an emerging industry focused on sustainable packaging solutions. A company operating in this sector, leveraging innovative technology and a unique business approach, may be undervalued compared to peers in conventional packaging sectors. This industry disruption presents an opportunity to invest in an undervalued asset.

Assessing The Leadership And Track Record Of A Company

The management team is critical to a company's success. Evaluating management can reveal insights into a company's ability to enhance shareholder value and handle challenging market conditions, helping to identify undervalued investment opportunities.

Examine the management team's track record in terms of past performance, strategic decisions, and execution. Consistent success suggests competent leadership and potential undervalued investment opportunities.

Evaluate the company's corporate governance and adherence to ethical practices. Effective governance reduces the risk of value destruction and increases the chances of finding undervalued investments.

Consider insider ownership and recent insider trading activities. High insider ownership and insider buying can indicate management's confidence in the company's undervalued potential.

Assess the quality and transparency of the company's communication with shareholders. A management team that regularly updates shareholders and demonstrates transparency can help identify undervalued investment opportunities.

For example, if you are analyzing a technology company led by a management team with a proven history of launching successful products and generating strong returns for investors, it may suggest an undervalued investment opportunity in the tech sector.

Weighing Potential Risks And Rewards Of An Investment

While pursuing undervalued investment opportunities can be profitable, investors must carefully assess associated risks. By considering various risk factors, they can better understand potential downsides and determine if potential rewards justify the risks.

Evaluate market and industry risks relevant to the investment opportunity, such as competition, regulatory changes, and technological disruptions. Assess whether potential returns compensate for these risks.

Analyze company-specific risks, including financial stability, reliance on key customers or suppliers, and operational challenges. Understanding these factors helps gauge the overall risk profile of the investment.

Assess the liquidity and volatility of the investment. Assets that are illiquid or in highly volatile markets may pose challenges in buying or selling at favorable prices.

Implement risk management strategies such as diversification across different asset classes, sectors, and geographical areas. Diversification helps mitigate potential losses from individual investment setbacks while benefiting from overall portfolio performance.

For instance, consider discovering an undervalued opportunity in a small-cap biotechnology firm. Despite potential high returns, it's crucial to grasp the inherent risks associated with early-stage drug development and regulatory approval processes.

Kerri Payne

Kerri Payne

5

Spreading Risk Across Different Asset Classes And Industries

Diversification is key to risk management and helps investors seize undervalued opportunities while spreading risk across various asset classes and industries.

Diversify across asset classes like equities, fixed income, real estate, and commodities. This strategy mitigates the risk of any one asset class while allowing exposure to undervalued opportunities in others.

Distribute investments across different industries to avoid overexposure to the risks of a single sector. This approach enables access to undervalued opportunities in various sectors while minimizing industry-specific risks.

Invest in different geographic regions or countries to diversify exposure to local market risks and take advantage of undervalued opportunities in international markets.

Regularly review and rebalance your portfolio to adapt to changing market conditions and maintain diversification. This practice helps capture new undervalued opportunities while managing risk.

For example, an investor seeking diversification might allocate investments across a variety of undervalued stocks, bonds, and real estate properties. By spreading investments across different asset classes and industries, the investor minimizes risk exposure while maximizing potential returns from undervalued opportunities.

Staying Updated On Current Events That Can Impact Investment Opportunities

Staying updated on current events and news is crucial for identifying undervalued investment opportunities. By monitoring economic, political, and industry-specific developments, investors can gain valuable insights into potential prospects.

Track key economic indicators like GDP growth, inflation rates, and unemployment figures. Economic news can highlight sectors or assets that may be undervalued due to prevailing economic conditions.

Geopolitical changes, such as trade agreements or political events, can influence specific industries or markets. Staying informed about geopolitical news allows you to identify undervalued opportunities or potential risks associated with these developments.

Monitor news and updates pertaining to specific industries or sectors of interest. Industry-specific news offers valuable insights into trends, market dynamics, and potential opportunities where investments may be undervalued.

Stay informed about news concerning companies under evaluation for investment. Developments like new product launches, mergers and acquisitions, or regulatory approvals can influence a company's valuation and present undervalued investment prospects.

For instance, if contemplating investments in healthcare, encountering news about potential shifts in government regulations could suggest undervalued opportunities within the sector. Keeping abreast of news and actively tracking developments enables investors to seize such opportunities effectively.

Kerri Payne

Kerri Payne

Conclusion

Identifying undervalued investment opportunities necessitates a comprehensive approach that integrates multiple strategies and techniques. By combining research on market trends, fundamental and technical analysis, financial statement review, industry disruption analysis, management evaluation, risk assessment, and diversification strategies, investors can enhance their chances of uncovering undervalued opportunities and achieving potential rewards.

Keep in mind that investing in undervalued opportunities involves risks, and thorough due diligence is crucial. Staying informed, exercising patience, and maintaining a long-term perspective can help position you for

Kerri Payne

success in identifying undervalued investments with the potential for significant returns.

www.ingramcontent.com/pod-product-compliance
Lightning Source LLC
Chambersburg PA
CBHW072055230526
45479CB00010B/1072